OHIO COUNTY PUBLIC LIBRARY
WHEELING, W. VA. 26003

## FOREWORD

"Frontiers of America" dramatizes some of the explorations and discoveries of real pioneers in simple, uncluttered text. America's spirit of adventure is seen in these early people who faced dangers and hardship blazing trails, pioneering new water routes, becoming Western heroes as well as legends, and building log forts and houses as they settled in the wilderness.

Although today's explorers and adventurers face different frontiers, the drive and spirit of these early pioneers in America's past still serve as an inspiration.

## ABOUT THE AUTHOR

During her years as a teacher and reading consultant in elementary schools, Mrs. McCall developed a strong interest in the people whose pioneering spirit built our nation. When she turned to writing as a full-time occupation, this interest was the basis for much of her work. She is the author of many books and articles for children and adults, and co-author of elementary school social studies textbooks.

*Frontiers of America*

# Settlers on a Strange Shore

by Edith McCall
pictures by Carol Rogers

**CHILDRENS PRESS®**
CHICAGO

Library of Congress Cataloging in
Publication Data
McCall, Edith S
  Settlers on a strange shore.
  1.  America—Disc. & explor.—Juvenile
fiction.    2.  U.S.—Hist.—Colonial period—
Juvenile fiction.   I.  Title
PZ7.M1229.Se       60-11154
ISBN 0-516-03367-0

Cover photograph courtesy
of James P. Rowan

**New 1980 Edition**
Copyright© 1960 by Regensteiner
Publishing Enterprises, Inc.
All rights reserved. Published
simultaneously in Canada.
Printed in the United States of America.
4 5 6 7 8 9 10 11 12 R

# IN THIS BOOK

Thirty Hungry Frenchmen.......... 7

Angry Indians at Fort Caroline...... 21

Spaniards at St. Augustine.......... 33

Mystery at Roanoke Island......... 45

Man Who Saved Jamestown........ 61

Capture of John Smith............. 77

Foothold in Virginia............... 92

Mayflower Driven to New England..100

Plymouth Stands Firm.............115

# THIRTY HUNGRY FRENCHMEN

The flags of France on two little ships were spots of color on the Atlantic Ocean.

They moved towards America, the land of mystery and shadow.

Seventy years had passed since Columbus had chanced upon islands not far from the land for which the ships were sailing. In those seventy years, many ships had crossed the sea. But most of them had gone farther south than the two little French ships were heading.

People had come to live in the new land, but not one white settlement was in all of the land which is now the United States of America. All the greatness of North America north of Mexico was still to come.

On the last day of April, 1562, a great shouting arose on the deck of the leading ship of the pair. High in the *crow's nest* atop the mainmast, a man pointed towards the west.

"Land ho!" he cried, and the shouting began. Soon every man could see what the watchman's long "spyglass" had shown him. The faint dark ridge between the sea and the sky became a strong line through the morning mist.

The sun's rays lighted it and the ships drew nearer. The men could see that the dark line was a forest beyond a white beach. To the men who watched, worn from ten weeks on the open sea, it promised adventure and riches and an interesting new life.

The ships turned northward as they drew near enough to the shore to see it clearly. Jean Ribaut, commander of the two ships, watched for an opening in the shore line which could mean a harbor for the ships.

The night watch took over and the ships still rode at sea, far enough from the shore to stay clear of dangerous rocks which the water could hide.

Dawn of May Day promised a clear, pleasant day. It found Jean Ribaut back on deck.

His fingers closed tightly on the heavy wooden rail as he thought of what this new month could bring to him and his men. A new life—or sudden death. Seven years earlier a French ship had sailed to Brazil in South America, with the same hopes he and his men now held. The colony they built there had not lasted a year. Did the soldiers and the young adventurers in Ribaut's own company have the strength to live in a raw, new land?

"I wonder," Ribaut said aloud. The soldiers were used to a rough life. But the young adventurers had always had servants to wait upon them. They called themselves "gentlemen," and a gentleman never did any hard work with his hands.

Ribaut lifted his glass to his eye again. What he saw put his questions about his men out of his mind, for there, just ahead, was the mouth of a great river. The river Ribaut saw was the one which would be marked on later maps as *St. John's River.* The Spanish called this land *Florida,* and said they owned it because some of their explorers had been there.

Ribaut checked his charts and maps. This river was not on the Spanish maps. His own country's ships had explored the St. Lawrence River and the coastline south almost as far as present Florida. The French flag had as much right here as the Spanish, Ribaut thought, for no one had settled the matter by planting a colony. That was what he planned to do.

He rolled up his maps and called the mate. The

ship was almost opposite the mouth of the wide river.

"Drop anchor here," he ordered. "See that sand bar across the river's mouth? Lower the small boats, and we'll go in them to find a way for the ships to go."

The next hour was an exciting one for the men who had so long been like prisoners on the little wooden ships. They lost no time in obeying the mate's orders, and happily scrambled into the small boats. They pulled hard on the oars to hurry the boats into the wide, sheltered basin of water beyond the sand bar.

"It's alive with big fish!" they cried. Their mouths watered at the thought of the good meals they would have after weeks of ship's food. Only moldy hard biscuits were left.

But they did not stop for fishing now. They pulled hard for shore, eager to feel good, solid earth beneath their feet. They could see sand beaches, making a pretty border for waving palms and moss-hung cedars beyond.

When the boats were only a few yards from shore, Ribaut held up his hand. "Wait!" he cried, and the rowing stopped.

Suddenly the beaches had become alive with almost naked men, their bodies bright with blue, red and black paint. The soldiers raised their clumsy guns.

"Hold your fire!" cried Ribaut. He saw that the strange-looking men were waving their arms in welcome. They carried no spears or the bows and arrows he had heard were common in the New World.

He waved in return, and ordered the men to put down their guns. "Row for shore," he told the sailors.

Soon the boats touched the sandy bottom. The Frenchmen, with great shouts, jumped from the boats and splashed through the shallow water to the beach. The Indians drew together back near the trees to see what these men from the white-winged bird of the sea would do.

Jean Ribaut had one thought. "Thank God for a safe journey!" In a few minutes, the excited men were on their knees on the sand, bowing their heads in prayer.

To the Indians, it seemed that these must be "children of the sun," for they had come from the edge of the sea where the sun came up each morning. Now they must be thanking their sun-father, just as they themselves gave thanks to the great sun for the blessings it brought. They waited quietly until the newcomers arose.

Then the chief gave an order. Indians who carried copper knives in leather belts about their waists hurried to the woods to cut boughs of the laurel trees. They arranged them in a circle. Then the chief stepped forward and, with his hands, made signs that he would like the visitors to sit down for a council.

Jean Ribaut nodded. But before he sat down, he asked two of his sailors to bring a chest from the small boat. He had expected to meet Indians, and knew from stories he had heard what he should do. He had the chest placed before him in the council circle. From it he took a robe of blue cloth. The French lily was embroidered all over it in thread of gold.

Ribaut held this robe out to the chief, using his hands to show that he meant it as a gift. He spread it out and put it around the chief's shoulders.

"It is beautiful!" The chief spoke excitedly, in his own tongue, of course, but Ribaut could tell what he meant. The dark hand stroked the cloth and

fingered it all during the strange talk that followed. Nothing was spoken that either could understand, and yet both Indians and Frenchmen knew that the talk was of friendship.

The next days, the men walked about the country, exploring. Ribaut found no way to move his ships over the sand bar, and so he did not feel that this was the place to build his fort and begin a colony.

Before they went on board the ships again to look further, he and his men met once more with the Indians. There was one thing he must learn before he left.

"The Golden Cities," he said to the chief, "where are the Golden Cities?" It took some time to make the chief understand what he meant.

There had been a story for years that somewhere in America there were seven golden cities, and the dream was slow in dying. The hope of finding these cities or of finding a river which could be a short cut from the Atlantic Ocean to the Pacific Ocean were two dreams held by each newcomer to the New World for many, many years.

14

At last the chief's face lost its puzzled look and he smiled and nodded.

"How far?" Ribaut asked them. "Where?"

The chief pointed to a boat and made paddling motions.

"You can get there by boat," Ribaut said, "but which way and how far?"

The chief seemed to understand. He pointed west. Then he made arm movements to show the rising and setting of the sun.

The men counted as the chief's arm made the swing twenty times.

"Twenty days' journey to the west by water," Ribaut said. "We shall move along until we find a river flowing from the west. This river comes from the south, the Indians tell me."

Before they left, Ribaut and his men gave more gifts to the Indians. They named the river the *River of May,* for the month in which they had found it. Then they brought from the ship a stone column on which were carved the arms of the King of France. They set the column firmly on the south bank of the river mouth, as a sign that the land belonged to France.

They said good-by to their new friends and sailed northward slowly. The new fort should be built at the mouth of the river from the west. Then some of the men could explore. Perhaps the river would be the one which was a passage to the China Sea. Ribaut's dreams grew stronger and brighter.

They explored the shore from time to time. At last the ships were opposite the mouth of another wide river, which seemed to come from the west. It was *Broad River* in what is now *South Carolina.*

"This looks most promising," Ribaut told his men. "This is where we will build our fort and begin a colony. But our supplies are low, and I must go back to France for more. Will thirty men of good will come forward? Those thirty will stay here to build a fort and hold the land for France. Those who stay are sure to gain fame and riches!"

Cries of "I'll stay!" were heard from almost everyone. Ribaut could choose among them the thirty he believed to be strongest in body and spirit.

A few days later, on the eleventh of June, the thirty men watched the ships disappear against the eastern sky. The restless ocean seemed to swallow them up. It was with a strange feeling that they turned their faces back to this wilderness where only the Indian was "at home." But work helped them forget their uneasiness, and soon the fort was started. A man named Albert had been named their leader.

"We shall need more food, long before the ships return," Albert told the men when the fort was almost finished. "How shall we get it?"

The thirty men looked at each other questioningly. A "gentleman" always had food set before him. He never did the work of a farmer, and he did not even know how to catch the many fish which could be seen in Broad River. But Indians had been to visit them here, too, and Ribaut had left them some trading goods.

"The Indians have plenty. They will give us some," they decided. The Indians near by not only hunted and fished, but they also grew corn, beans and squash in their cleared fields.

Several times the Indians near the fort shared with the white men. But their new crops were not yet ripe, and they did not have enough for themselves after they had given so much away.

"To the south there are two chiefs who are rich in the yellow corn," the Indians told the Frenchmen.

"Go to them, men from over the sea, and they will have food for you."

The good Indians even offered to guide the men to the villages. In small boats, the men followed the guides' canoe through streams and lakes that lay not far from the ocean. Sometimes the boats had to be carried overland, but not far or often. The journey ended at a village on the Savannah River in what is now Georgia.

The Frenchmen gave the Indians beads and other small gifts, and the Indians loaded one of their boats with corn and vegetables. They went back to the fort and put their treasure into the storehouse.

A day or two later, the men arose in the morning to see only a smoking, black pile where the storehouse had been. Again they went to the village on the Savannah.

"So long as we have food, our friends from over the sea shall not go hungry," the chief told them, and again they went home with a loaded boat.

There was nothing to do, then, but wait for Ribaut to return. The "gentlemen" gave no thought to clearing fields where they would plant in the spring, or to doing any other work. They ate and slept, and soon they quarreled.

Weeks turned into months. Each day seemed hotter than the one before. Tempers grew short. The woods no longer seemed to hold adventure. They were a prison wall, and the river was a mocking mirror, no longer a roadway to riches. And still Ribaut did not return.

Albert gave orders but no one obeyed. One day he hanged a man for not obeying. The men took sides, for and against their leader. One night Albert was murdered.

A man named Nicolas became the leader.

"We are leaving here," he said. "Ribaut left us tools, iron and a forge. We can cut trees to get wood, and build ourselves a ship."

The work gave them new life. At last their patchwork ship, made watertight with Spanish moss and pine pitch stuffed into its cracks, sailed eastward, only to lie in the middle of the ocean waiting for wind to fill the sails. The starving, almost mad crew was found there by an English ship which carried them home.

The fort in the wilderness rotted away. But Jean Ribaut, unable to get the supplies his men had needed, held to his dream. He would be back.

# ANGRY INDIANS AT FORT CAROLINE

Two years and a month had passed since the French ships had come to the River of May for the first time. The chief's beautiful blue robe had worn thin and the gold threads were broken, but still he talked of his friends, the "children of the sun."

Then, on a day in June of 1564, a runner came into the chief's lodge.

"The bird ships return, oh great Chief Satouriona!" he cried. "The men from the land where the sun lives are coming again!"

Satouriona jumped up. He must be at the beach to meet his old friends. All the people of the village went with him. This time there were three ships riding on the waves. Again the flag they flew was that of France.

As he saw the newcomers lowering boats to come ashore, Satouriona, with his two sons, set out in a canoe to meet his old friends while his people danced a dance of welcome on the beach.

When Satouriona was near to the boat in which

the French leader rode, he saw that it was not his old friend, Ribaut. For a moment, he was sad. Then he saw that this leader was dressed as Ribaut had been. He was probably his brother, come to see his old friend in Ribaut's place.

"Antipola! Antipola!" he cried in welcome, and the Indians on the shore took up the cry. The French leader, whose name was Laudonniere, was pleased at their joy. He called out greetings in return, and French boat and Indian canoe went to the beach side by side.

"Come!" Satouriona signalled happily. He took Laudonniere to the top of a little rise. There stood the stone column Ribaut's men had placed two years before. Then the Indians invited the white men to a feast.

Laudonniere took gifts with him when he went to the feast. But Satouriona wanted to give more than he took. He held out a pretty stone to his new friend.

"Why, it is silver!" Laudonniere said. Satouriona was pleased to see his friend's eyes light with joy. He happily told Laudonniere where it came from in answer to the French leader's signalled question.

"Thimagoas! Thimagoas!" he said, and pointed south. He made Laudonniere understand that the Thimagoas were Satouriona's enemies. The silver and some bits of gold he showed Laudonniere were prizes of war.

"We will go together to see the Thimagoas," Laudonniere told him. "My men will help your men fight your enemies. Together, we shall win all their gold and silver."

Satouriona was not sure why the white man was so interested in the silver and the gold, but it pleased him that his gifts were liked. Most of all, he was pleased to have the white man's promise to help him fight his enemy, the Thimagoas.

Laudonniere was anxious to learn more about the precious metals, but he knew that his first business was the colony.

"I see no better place to build a fort than right here," he decided. He was standing on a bluff, not far from the stone column. In his bright silk clothes and his hat with the great feather on it, he looked strange against the wilderness of forest and marsh behind him. But with the Indians as his friends, he gave little thought to the dangers.

He stroked his pointed beard and looked towards the ocean on his right and then to the River of May on his left. Yes, this was the spot for a colony.

Fort Caroline arose there. It was three-sided, with one side set along the river bank. There the men set logs on end to build a palisade. On the other two sides, they dug a deep ditch which filled with water from the river. The earth from the ditches helped form the fort walls. At the corners, large earth platforms were built, and the cannons were brought ashore and placed on these. Ammunition was stored in a room under one of them.

The center was left open for a parade ground. Houses and storerooms were built along the sides. Laudonniere and his officers had a house two-stories high, with balconies, on the side towards the river. In his mind, the leader could already see the houses which would be built outside the fort as the settlement grew and women and children came to join the men.

Satouriona called often to know when the white men would be ready to go to fight the Thimagoas.

"As soon as our houses have roofs," Laudonniere told him one day. An hour later, most of the Indian

men were cutting grasses and tying them into bundles to make thatch for the roofs. In two days' time, the roofs were finished.

"Now?" asked Satouriona.

"I would like to have my lieutenant, Ottigny, go there first, to learn more of the Thimagoas," Laudonniere said then.

The next day, several Indians were paddling their canoe up the River of May, followed by Ottigny and a few soldiers. They headed south, hemmed in by tropical forests on both sides of the river.

There were palms, great oaks, maples, and cypress trees with their knobby "knees" sticking out of the water. Off in the forest, wildcats screamed and birds called loudly. Now and then a soft-eyed deer watched motionless as the men passed. Alligators sunned themselves on the banks, and great turtles lay in the mud. To the Frenchmen, it was a strange world.

When they had gone about sixty miles up the river, the guides became greatly excited.

"Thimagoa! Thimagoa!" they cried, and pointed to three canoes not far away. But, as the French boats drew near, the Indians in the three canoes took to the woods. As the Frenchmen stepped ashore, they made no move to follow. Their Indian guides pulled at their swords, as if to get the Frenchmen to use the swords on the Thimagoas.

But Ottigny just stood and asked questions about where the village was located, letting the Thimagoas disappear completely from sight.

"We'll forget this business of fighting the Thimagoas," he told his own men. "If we make friends with them, perhaps they'll trade their silver and gold for our glass beads. We'll learn where the metals come from."

So began a plan which was to lose for the Frenchmen the most valuable thing they had—the friendship of Chief Satouriona and his men.

They returned to the Thimagoas' village without their guides, after telling Satouriona they were getting ready for the fight and that he should do likewise. The Thimagoas seemed not to have any more gold or silver.

"It is in the village of the men of the mountains," their chief, Mollua, told the Frenchmen. "But the tribes there are my enemies. Go with me to fight

28

against them, and you shall have a heap of gold and silver two feet high!"

Ottigny, seeming to forget the promise already made to Satouriona, agreed to be Mollua's friend and help fight the mountain people. He went back to the fort to report.

While he had been gone, Satouriona had gathered together several chiefs and five hundred braves to go to fight the Thimagoas. The woods were alive with painted warriors.

"We are ready," Satouriona told Laudonniere.

"Wait awhile," the French leader said. "We are not quite ready for the battle."

The chief became angry. That night, the Frenchmen saw a great fire near the river. They went close enough to see the warriors and chiefs gathered around it. The light of the flames on their painted bodies, and their long black hair, often covered with headdresses of the heads and skins of wolves and bears, made them look very fierce.

Two great kettles of water were beside the fire. After the Indians had gone through a long ceremony, Satouriona sprinkled all his men with water from one kettle. Then he turned the other kettle so that the water spilled onto the fire and put it out.

He cried, "So may the blood of our enemies be poured out and their lives ended!"

In the morning, the Indians went to war without the Frenchmen. They came back in a few days with many scalps and thirteen prisoners.

Laudonniere made his greatest mistake then. He took two of the prisoners and returned them to Mollua, to get the Thimagoa chief's friendship. His soldiers helped Mollua in an attack on the mountain tribe.

The mountain Indians fled at the sight of the bearded Frenchmen with their armor and their roaring sticks that could kill. The village was burned. But Mollua found no heap of gold for the Frenchmen. Laudonniere could not find out where the gold was mined. Disappointed, he went back to the fort.

Satouriona's men hated the French now. The Frenchmen dared not walk in the woods. They sat inside their fort most of the time, growing hungrier each day. The Thimagoas would give them little food, and they had not tried to grow any for themselves.

Winter passed and the spring of 1565 came. Still

no "gentleman" turned a spadeful of earth. Each day became worse than the one before, for now the storehouses were empty.

One day, in August, the lookout on the ocean side saw seven ships coming from over the ocean. The men did not know whether to be afraid or happy. If the ships were those of their enemy, the Spanish, who were known to be near, they would all be killed. If they were French ships, there would be new life for them all.

Laudonniere was ill. From his bed, he listened for sounds that would tell their fate. At last, when it seemed he must get up from his bed and find out for himself, the cry came, "It is Jean Ribaut!"

Laudonniere sighed weakly. "We are saved!" he murmured.

New spirit went all through the fort. Tents were pitched for the many men, women and children who had come to join the American colony. Fort Caroline would soon be a little city in the New World, the first north of Mexico.

But even as houses were begun outside the walls of the fort, something was happening a few miles to the south which would cut their dreams short. On the fourth of September, they had the first hint of trouble to come. The evening light showed a great ship coming near. And from its mast flew the flag of Spain.

# SPANIARDS AT ST. AUGUSTINE

Ribaut had waited a long time for the day when he would head that fleet of seven ships back to America. He hoped that this time all would go well, and New France would have a firm beginning in America. The men, women and children he was taking to Fort Caroline would build a fine town.

Just as Ribaut set sail from France another set of ships was being fitted out to go to America. But this fleet was at a Spanish port, and the flag of Spain waved from the masts. The ships were under the command of Pedro Menendez, who was planning to start a settlement in Florida.

News of Ribaut's seven shiploads of colonists reached the king of Spain just as Menendez was setting sail.

"Call Menendez back!" he ordered. "We shall send a stronger force and drive the French away. Florida is our land, not theirs."

Soon Menendez was on his way again, with more than 4,600 people on thirty-four ships. They carried with them everything they thought would be needed for a colony in America, including plenty of horses, sheep and hogs. In a few months, more ships were to follow with another 1,500 men.

When at last he saw Florida's shores, Menendez felt that the first thing he should do was to find Ribaut and his French colony. In his flagship, he sailed northward along the coast. So it was that on the fourth of September, 1565, the French saw the big Spanish ship coming toward their harbor. Menendez had found what he was looking for.

But he was not yet ready to attack Fort Caroline. His warship tried to catch up with three of the smaller French ships which moved out of the harbor as the big Spanish ship came near. But the French ships were too fast, and Menendez ordered the ship to turn back south to join the other Spanish ships.

The place the Spaniards chose for their fort was only about thirty-five or forty miles from Fort Caroline. The fact that an Indian village was there already did not bother them at all. They scared the Indians away with their big guns, and took the largest of the Indian lodges for their first headquarters. The lodge was built with tree trunks for its walls

and a roof of bent limbs thatched with palmetto leaves. The Spaniards dug a ditch around it and threw the dirt against the sides to strengthen it. This was the beginning of the settlement they named *St. Augustine.*

While the Spanish were doing this, the French up at Fort Caroline were worried.

"They have thirty-four ships and many, many cannon," their scouts reported. "But they do not have a fort as strong as ours."

Jean Ribaut and some of the officers went into Laudonniere's room in the officer's house in the fort to talk about what would be best to do. They were both sure that the Spanish would not wait long to attack. But that was the only thing on which they agreed.

Laudonniere, still sick, could think only of how the men could make the fort stronger. "We can hold out against them here if we repair the walls," he said. "There are enough men now to defend Fort Caroline."

But Jean Ribaut felt that they must choose the time of attack themselves.

"We could attack them from the sea so suddenly

that most of their ships would soon be ours," he said.

"Why not march by land and burn their fort?" another officer asked.

"If we had plenty of men we could do both," said Ribaut. "But the wilderness is strange to us, and they would learn we were coming long before we reached them. I believe a sea attack is best."

Laudonniere rose up from his bed. "But what about Fort Caroline? How can we defend it if they attack, with all our soldiers away?" he asked.

Ribaut said, "We shall leave a small company here. But don't worry. We shall be back before the Spanish have time to get started."

There was an argument, then. Some of the men felt that Ribaut's plan was too risky. But when a vote was taken, it was in favor of the surprise attack from the sea.

On the morning of the tenth, the seven French ships sailed south, carrying most of the able-bodied men from Fort Caroline.

Laudonniere, too sick to go, lay in his bed worrying about the broken-down palisades of Fort Caroline and the women and children with their houses only partly built. They would have to take shelter inside the fort if attack came. The few men in the fort would have to work very hard to repair the walls. Some of them were sick, too.

Laudonniere sighed. He got off the bed and stood up. His knees buckled a bit and he sat down again. It was no use.

All could have gone well if a hurricane had not been working its way towards the Florida coast that day. Ribaut's ships fought high winds and great waves all the way down to the place where Menendez' ships lay tossing about at anchor. But the French felt the bad weather would help them in their surprise attack.

And then it hit. The French ships were suddenly tipped so that their sails almost touched the water. There was a quick scurrying of men on the rope ladders. They fought with ropes and canvas as the downpour of rain came. No man could hear another man's voice over the shrieking of the wind and the creaking of the masts.

In the Indian lodge turned into a fort, Menendez waited for the end of the storm. His own ships were anchored and tied inside the harbor.

"French ships sighted," the report came to him

from his guards. "They are in trouble in the storm."

When the rains and the winds at last quieted, the guards reported wrecked French ships. They were not sure what had become of the French soldiers and sailors.

"We shall not wait for them to be found," Menendez decided. "Before they can make their way back to their fort, we shall attack it. That will be an end to France's colony on Spanish land."

Menendez decided to make his attack from land. Soon five hundred armed men were picking their way through the swampy land. The forty miles seemed an endless journey through mud that sucked at their boots and made each step a battle. There was no dry place to camp so soon after the hurricane, and the men were ready to give up long before they reached Fort Caroline.

The officers argued that the way ahead was shorter than the way back, and soon they would be drinking the Frenchmen's wines. So on they went, and on the night of September 19, they were one mile from Fort Caroline. The officers ordered a rush on the fort in the morning.

In the gray morning light, death came to French

40

hopes for a colony in Florida. A few of the French people who were at Fort Caroline escaped into the woods. The breaks in the walls made it easy for the Spanish soldiers to get inside. The few able-bodied men who were there had no hope of holding out against five hundred Spanish soldiers. Those who could, including Laudonniere, escaped into the woods.

Some of them offered to surrender to the Spanish. Their answer was a slash of the sword. Those still in the fort were hanged. Only when they were sure the French could never retake Fort Caroline did Menendez' main army leave. A handful of men were left in the French fort.

Two French ships in the harbor took all the people on board who had a chance to get to them. One of these was Laudonniere. Then, before the Spanish could stop them, they opened sails and headed for France.

Menendez was ready now to deal with the shipwrecked Frenchmen. He found groups of them camped along the beaches as they tried to make their way back to Fort Caroline. To each group, he made an offer of peace if they would surrender. He led the men a few at a time to a low spot behind a hill on a lonely beach. There he killed the prisoners in cold blood.

Most of the French colonists were of the religious group called Huguenots. This was at a time when all Europe was upset by religious arguments. The Spanish believed they had a right to kill anyone who did not believe exactly as they did, even though they all called themselves "Christians."

"It is not as Frenchmen we kill you, but as Huguenots," Menendez told the surrendering Frenchmen.

Jean Ribaut's dreams of New France ended there on that lonely stretch of beach behind the hill.

A few months later, an angry French sailor anchored his ship not far from Fort Caroline, still held by a handful of Spanish soldiers. The story of the terror of September 20, 1565, had reached his ears in France. He went ashore to talk with Satouriona, who had found the Spanish even less to his liking than Laudonniere's soldiers. Satouriona had been happy to see the return of his old friend, Jean Ribaut, who had given him the beautiful blue robe.

Satouriona was ready and willing to attack Fort

Caroline by land while the French ship fired at it from the harbor. The plans were made without the Spanish soldiers knowing about it.

Fort Caroline fell again, but this time it was the Spanish who were killed inside its walls. The Frenchmen, feeling that they had done a little to even the score, sailed away. About fifty years would pass before there would be a lasting French colony in North America, and it would be far from Florida. It would be in the north on the St. Lawrence River, where Samuel Champlain would found Quebec in 1608.

Pedro Menendez had been back in Spain when the French sailors and Satouriona attacked his men at Fort Caroline. When he returned he rebuilt the fort. When the land on which it stood began to wash away, he built another fort farther inland.

Long after Satouriona was dead, fighting went on in the land the white men took from his people. Spanish, French, Indians, English and Americans all fought there at one time or another. Now the largest city of Florida, Jacksonville, stands near the mouth of St. John's River. Only a few monuments are there to remind people of Jean Ribaut's dreams.

But St. Augustine went on growing. Menendez built a strong fort, and a city grew around it. The Spanish "gentlemen" brought slaves to Florida to farm the land. By trading with other Spanish colonies, the colony of St. Augustine became stronger year by year. It is the city of St. Augustine today, oldest city in the United States of America.

# MYSTERY AT ROANOKE ISLAND

For twenty years, St. Augustine stood alone as the only white settlement in all the land north of Mexico in the great New World. It looked as though New Spain would reach as far north as Canada, as the Spanish people claimed it did.

But in 1585, the first step was taken which was to change the pattern. Seven little ships, flying the flag of England were heading for the New World. The year before, English ships had sailed into Pamlico Sound, off the coast of what is now North Carolina. The English travelers had gone on shore.

There they saw great, tall trees, eighteen feet around the trunk. The many different kinds of plant and animal life surprised and pleased them. But the spicy smell in the air was what charmed them most. It awoke old dreams of a land of spices and gold and jewels.

They camped on an island which they named Roanoke. There the Indians welcomed them. They invited the white visitors to a feast of fish, venison, boiled roots, fruits, a tea made of wild ginger and sassafras roots, and the juice of the wild grape.

"A wonderful land," the sailors reported when they were back in England. Sir Walter Raleigh, who owned the ships, began to plan a colony for Roanoke Island.

"The land is ours," he told people who reminded him that Spain and France both claimed North America. "John Cabot explored its coast before the French and Spanish ships went there."

He fitted out the seven ships and found people who were willing to go to America to make homes in the new land. Sir Richard Grenville was to be the commander of the fleet and the colony.

Through April and May, June and July, the little wooden ships moved across the great sea, or rocked on the waves as they waited for winds to fill their sails. On a day in early August, the colonists saw for the first time the land of the New World.

Sir Richard had charts and maps to help him find Roanoke Island. The people went ashore there on August 17, 1585.

The Indians danced and sang and invited the newcomers to a feast.

Only a few days later, Sir Richard began to get the ships ready to go back to England.

"You will need more supplies to get through the first year," he told the people. "If the weather is right, I shall be back with them before winter, or by next spring at the latest." Soon he was gone, and the little group, one hundred eight men, was left alone in a land which had little in it to make them feel at home.

The Indians were surprised to see the ships sail away without taking all their white visitors. Why were these strange men cutting down their trees and building houses on their island? The ceremonies they held now were not feasts of joy at the coming of the white man. When winter came and Sir Richard had not come back, the Indians gave the settlers very little of their food.

Spring came, and every day the colonists watched for sails coming up Pamlico Sound. April and May went by, and then at last on a June day, the call went out, "A sail! A sail!"

But the ships were not those of Sir Richard. They carried no supplies to leave at Roanoke, or new colonists to join the men who had been there almost a year. Sir Francis Drake was in command of the ships. The ships carried the flag of England, and England was heaven in the minds of the colonists.

They did not know that Sir Richard's ships were almost there, bringing more colonists and the much needed food. They went on board Sir Francis' ships and passed Sir Richard a few days later, but too far away to be seen.

Sir Richard arrived at Roanoke Island and looked around at the deserted cabins.

"What could have happened to our people," he said.

"If they found it so hard, I don't want to stay either," said one of the new colonists. Many agreed. But Sir Richard found fifteen men who loved adventure who were willing to stay. Again Sir Richard went back to England with promises to return.

When Sir Francis' ships reached England with the colonists aboard, Sir Walter Raleigh was very unhappy. He had great hopes that England would some day own a large part of North America and would have many riches from the New World. Sir Francis Drake's report that, just before he picked up the colonists, he had set fire to St. Augustine was

good news. That would slow down the Spanish in their plans.

Quickly Sir Walter set about getting a new group of people to go to America. This time he allowed the men to take their wives and children, thinking that families would make it a stronger colony. A good man named John White was to be the leader. Sir Walter talked a long time with John White before the ships sailed.

"Perhaps Roanoke Island is not the best place for a colony, since there has been trouble there," he told him. "If the last group of men who went there are not doing well, go to some place on the mainland."

John White had good reason to do all he could to be sure his one hundred twenty-one settlers had a good start. One of them was his daughter, Eleanor, who had been married to Ananias Dare a few months before.

The ships sailed early in the summer of 1587. The weather was good, but even at its calmest the ocean was never quiet. Eleanor White Dare stood often at the rail, wondering if she was wise to have come. Before fall, she and Ananias would have a child.

"Do not worry yourself," Ananias told her. "A

child born in the New World will have a wonderful life. He will be free from all the troubles of the old."

Eleanor turned to the sea which seemed never to end. No matter which way she looked, she saw only the rolling waves and the endless sky. Ananias and her father thought only of adventure and freedom. To a woman, it was different. The July sun suddenly seemed blinding, and she went below.

One day in the middle of July, the sailor in the crow's nest gave the cry, "Land ho! Land ho!"

The long journey was nearly over. The ship nosed into Pamlico Sound, and on July 22 anchor was dropped off Roanoke Island. The sailors set to work at once to get the one hundred twenty-one people and all their baggage and supplies on shore.

John White was eager to find the fifteen men who had stayed on from Sir Richard's company.

"Come, Ananias," he said to his son-in-law. "Search the island. Surely they are not far away."

The two men and a few others of the company crossed to the west side of the island. There they saw Indians fishing in a shallow bay. A net closed in part of the bay, and some of the Indians stood in the water, catching the trapped fish with long spears.

Other Indians in a dugout canoe came close to take the catch.

The Indians saw the newcomers standing on the shore, looking uncomfortable in their English clothes. The Indians in the canoe paddled towards them, and the spearmen stopped to watch. English visitors on Roanoke Island had become quite common. The Indians had learned enough about them not to dance in joy at their coming.

They beached their canoe, and began a long talk with the newcomers, mostly in hand signs. John White asked where the fifteen white men were. The Indians either did not know, or they pretended not to know.

"Take me to your chief," John White said. One of the Indians led the way to a village, not far away. The others returned to their fishing.

The Englishmen saw a little group of houses in a clearing, with a small cornfield and vegetable garden near by.

"The houses look like dark loaves of bread from a baker's oven," Ananias said. The huts were made of the trunks of young trees bent into U-shape with the ends in the ground. Poles and grapevine held pieces of tree bark in place to close the walls. There was a low doorway on the side of each "loaf."

A few Indians worked in or near the village. Some women worked at a cooking fire near the largest house at the center of the village. Other women were treating deerskins. A group of men were working at the edge of the woods beyond the village.

The visitors waited after the Indian went inside the largest house. They looked about with interest. They saw that the men at the edge of the woods were making a dugout canoe. The blackened stump of a tree stood near by, and it looked as if the men had brought down the log on which they were working mostly by burning it. They were shaping it that way, too. Where the fires had burned out, they were scraping away the charred wood with large flat shells.

In a few minutes, their guide came back. He motioned for them to follow him inside the lodge. Women sat along the sides of the room, at the end, on a raised platform covered with skins, sat the chief. He was wearing a robe made of feathers, and many shell and bone ornaments.

Again, John White "spoke" in sign language.

54

Again, his answer was neither friendly nor unfriendly, but it told him nothing. The chief would say only that the white men had been on the island and now they were not.

Discouraged, the newcomers offered gifts to the chief and then turned away. The chief quickly sent the guide for a jar of corn to give the white men in return.

"I think we should move to another place," John White said, when he had called all the people together.

"Yes," said the others. "It would give us a fresh start."

White asked the ship's captains to move his people to the mainland. But the captains shook their heads.

"We were paid to bring you to Roanoke Island," they said. "That is what we have done. We sail back in the morning."

All the ships left but one. The people decided to make the best of things, and began repairing the huts of earlier colonists.

John White said, "If I am to bring you the supplies you will need, I must go back to England soon.

But before I go, I want to know that you will be safe. We are going to set up a strong wall around the houses."

When the work was almost finished, White got ready to go.

"When I come back, we'll plant crops for ourselves. Virginia will be a strong arm of England in a new land," he told his people.

"Virginia" was the name given to all the land which the queen had given to Sir Walter Raleigh's company.

White told the colonists that if they had to leave Roanoke, to leave a cross as a sign if they were in trouble. Then he said good-by to his daughter, Eleanor Dare.

"Take good care of my grandchild until I get back," he said as he kissed her. Then he and the last of the ships were gone.

The grandchild, a girl, was born two weeks later, on August 18, 1587. Two days after her birth she was christened.

"We'll name her Virginia, in honor of our new land," her parents decided. And so Virginia Dare began her life as no English child had ever done before—in the wilderness of the New World. Her parents hoped her life in the new land would grow better each year.

But no one knows what kind of life Virginia Dare had, or if she grew to be a woman. John White could not get the supplies and ships he needed as soon as he was back in England. It was two years before he could set sail for America again. And when he reached Roanoke Island, there was no sign of Virginia Dare, her parents, or any of the other colonists.

Anxiously, he went from one deserted cabin to another. Weeds grew tall about them, almost blocking the doorways. Before he looked inside any of them, his heart told him it was no use.

"There must be some sign—some message to tell me what happened," he thought, and went on searching. In one cabin he found a chest he had left there. His papers and maps were on the dirt floor, moldy and dirty.

All he and the sailors who helped him search could find was a word carved on a tree, "CROATOAN," and on another "CRO." There was no

cross, the sign they had agreed upon to show trouble.

The Indians on the island would tell them nothing except there were Indians on an island twenty miles to the south called Croatoans."

"Then we'll go there," John White said. The sailors, anxious to be on their way back to England, shrugged their shoulders. But they raised the anchor and set sail for Croatoan Island.

Perhaps John White might have found his people if he had reached the island. No one will ever know, for so bad a storm came up that the ship was almost wrecked. The captain set sail back for England, and broken-hearted John White had no choice but to go along. By this time, England was at war with Spain, and colonies in the New World were forgotten.

Some say the colonists were murdered. Others say they lived with the Croatoan Indians for many years. There are stories of a beautiful white girl living among the Indians. Not many years ago, a stone was found on which was scratched, "Anye Englishman shew John White Govr Via." But some say this stone was carved and buried as a trick. No one can say for sure what happened. The mystery of the "Lost Colony of Roanoke Island" is buried in the past of the brave New World.

## MAN WHO SAVED JAMESTOWN

For twenty years more, the countries of Europe were too busy with wars to do much about their colonies in the New World. But on the night of April 26, 1607, three ships dropped anchor off Cape Henry on the Virginia shoreline. Morning's light showed that they carried the flag of England.

The next day, the three ships went on westward. They had found the south end of Chesapeake Bay, and were carefully moving in toward the James River. They crossed to the north edge of the wide river's mouth. There they dropped anchor, and found the spot so pleasant they named it Point Comfort.

Soon a small boat was lowered from each of the two smaller ships, and the captains of the ships, with a few other men, were rowed alongside the largest ship, the *Susan Constant.*

"Come aboard, gentlemen," called Captain Christopher Newport. He was captain of the *Susan Constant,* and was the only leader the colonists had during the journey. But this evening would change that. The men were coming to a meeting at which the colonists' sealed orders would be opened. The papers would have the names of seven men who were to be the council which would govern the colony.

When the men were all gathered in his quarters on the ship, Captain Newport took the chest which held the orders and unlocked it. From the chest he took the folded paper, held closed with sealing wax.

"Gentlemen," he said as he broke the seal, "you all know that these names were chosen before we left England. I am sure that they shall be those of the most able men among us, and we shall all stand by the choice."

He began to read. "Christopher Newport." No one seemed surprised to hear their captain's name at the head of the list. "Bartholomew Gosnold, John Ratcliffe."

Again heads nodded. They were captains of the other two ships. Three more names followed. "Edward Wingfield, John Martin, George Kendall."

Captain Newport seemed surprised at the seventh name. He looked at Captain Ratcliffe as he said, "And John Smith."

"John Smith!" Captain Ratcliffe jumped to his feet. "Why he's in irons this minute! John Smith would have himself be king of Virginia, if he had the chance! No, I say! He shall not be on the council!"

Voices rose until the little cabin seemed like a beehive. Captain Newport rapped for order. When it was more quiet he said, "It is true that Captain Smith is held as a prisoner. But he is a man of many ideas, and most of them are good. I don't believe he intended to try to take over leadership of this colony. It is just his natural way to speak up when he has an idea. Now, our king and the London Company saw fit to name him to the council, and he shall have his place there. Goodnight, gentlemen!"

Down in the hold of one of the ships, John Smith moved restlessly. He knew that the ship had anchored and that the Virginia shores had been reached. He gave a useless, impatient tug at the chain which held him in the dark prison, bound to a hateful band around his ankle.

A fine way for a man who had been a brave soldier—yes, and a hero, too—to be coming to the New World! Smith banged his fist against the wall and

kicked at the iron chain. He knew nothing of his name being on the list of council members. He supposed that he would be sent back to England in this same dark hole. And all because he had told Ratcliffe a better way to handle some of the men on the ship!

A day or two later, as the ships moved on again up the river, John Smith was greatly surprised to find himself free. Captain Christopher Newport had sent for him. He told Smith of his place on the council, and that there was to be a meeting to elect a president.

Captain Smith came to the meeting but when it came time for the vote, his was not counted. Most of the members wanted Christopher Newport to be president, but the ship captains knew that they might have to leave the colony to go after supplies.

"Choose a man who can stay at the colony to attend to affairs here," he said. Edward Wingfield was elected.

President Wingfield read the London Company's orders about the place on which the settlement should be built. It was to be at the mouth of a river which looked as if it could lead to the other side of

America, so that trade could go on with ships on the China Sea.

"How far do you think that is?" one asked.

"There is a ridge of mountains, we are told, about one hundred miles away. The newest maps show a river cutting through somewhat to the north and west. It leads to a great sea, which in turn leads to the Sea of China farther to the west," Captain Newport told the council. "This great river-mouth we have found could easily be that river, for it is wide and deep."

President Wingfield read also that ships should be able to tie close to the colony for easy shipping of goods, and that the land should not be too low, so as to be healthful.

When they thought they had found a good place, on a peninsula on the north bank of the James, they tied their ships right to the trees on the bank. They felt sure the James River, as they named it, could easily be the river that led to the sea.

But John Smith looked over the place with the practiced eye of a soldier who had camped in many places.

"There is swampland just over the rise," he said.

"This place is not high enough ground to be healthful."

In the voting that followed, Smith's vote was again not counted. Three were against this place and three for it. President Wingfield decided that they had looked far enough.

With a place for the colony chosen, the sea-worn men set to work with a will. The gentlemen who made up a large part of the company of one hundred five men, were not sure of how to go about the work. But the four carpenters and a few other workmen showed the way. Among the best at swinging an ax was Captain John Smith.

They set up tents for shelter until houses could be built. Some of the sailors made fish nets so that they could get fish to eat, and a few men started a garden, hopefully planting seeds they had brought from England.

The first trees cut down had to be for lumber to go back on the ship so that the London Company could sell it to help pay expenses of the colony. Tall pines were cut and squared off and split into rough boards, needed for house building in England.

"I shall be sailing soon," Captain Newport said.

"But before I leave, I want to see that a fort is begun. I've seen the Indians watching us, and I think we should have a safe place in case they decide to be unfriendly."

"Oh, no," said President Wingfield. "If we build a fort, they will think we mean to be unfriendly. It will make them angry."

John Smith spoke up, as usual. "You are wrong, Mr. Wingfield. The Indians want us to show how strong we are. If we do not, they will show their strength against us."

There was another argument, but in the end, Captain Newport's wishes were carried out. A fort was begun, and most of the men were pleased. They could sleep more soundly, knowing that a log wall with a locked gate was between them and the Indians. A three-sided fort was soon well along.

Before he left, Captain Newport made a trip up the James River to learn more about it. He took John Smith and a few other men with him. They went as far as a waterfall without seeing any end to the river. This could easily be the river to the sea.

He had one more thing to do. He asked President Wingfield to call a council meeting, and before it was over, he had made the members agree to John Smith's right to vote.

"Smith has more good sense than any six others," the old captain told them. "Listen to his ideas, and think over what he says."

The captain sailed away then, with promises to be back with suppiles as soon as he could. Something seemed to leave the colony with the ship, for the men chose to do nothing all day but lie around. It was hot weather, and a few of them were sick, but most of them were just lazy.

"Gentlemen, we cannot live in these tents for long," President Wingfield said. "We should be cutting trees for houses."

"A gentleman doesn't work with his hands. We'll get servants to do the work," was all the answer he got.

"In this warm weather, we don't need houses anyway," said one, and most of them agreed. Wingfield himself did not know how to swing an ax. He secretly agreed that a gentleman should do no work with his hands. But there were no servants to do the work. Even the garden, so hopefully planted in May, wilted in the summer heat and gave up.

Of the men on the council, only John Smith did part of the hard work. He alone seemed to worry about the food supply which was growing smaller each day.

He spoke to President Wingfield. "Order some of the men to go with me, and we'll trade with the Indians for food."

But Indians attacked the fort, and no one would go out with Smith. Then came worse trouble. Man after man became ill, and death came to the colony for the first time. Captain Gosnold died in August. Thomas Wotton, who knew as much about medicine as anyone of his day, did his best to cure the men, but it was a losing fight. September saw many more dead.

John Smith, weak from his own struggle with the sickness, saw the tired Wotton feeding men too weak to help themselves.

"I'll help," he said. From then on, he worked at nursing the others. John Ratcliffe, who had put Smith into chains not many months earlier, found himself being fed and washed by the big soldier whose rough hands held him so gently.

"Smith, you're not such a bad fellow after all," he said.

As the first cool days of fall came, the men faced another problem. Their food supply was gone. Almost half of their number had died, and more were dying because there was not good food to bring back their strength.

President Wingfield seemed not to care what happened. He did little but watch for the return of Captain Newport's ships.

John Smith took it upon himself to call the council together. There were only four members now—Ratcliffe, Smith, Martin and Kendall.

"You should be president, Smith," said Captain Ratcliffe. "If it weren't for your help, Martin and I would be dead. You nursed us through our illness. Take the presidency."

"No," said Smith, and no one could change his mind. John Ratcliffe was elected president. But Smith was quick to speak up with ideas of what to do until the ship came.

"Whatever you say," said Ratcliffe. "You seem to know more about how to live in this awful wilderness than any of the rest of us."

Kendall said, "I'll not take orders from a man who arrived here in irons." He walked away. Later, he was seen with Wingfield and a man named Archer. They seemed to be trying to get first one man and then another to join them in some secret plan.

John Smith paid no attention to these secret moves, but set the men who were strong enough to work to cutting marsh grasses to make roofing thatch. He and others cut trees and began the framework of several houses.

The men who had been working hard were very angry when they found what Kendall and his group had been up to. Their plan was discovered when all the food in the camp disappeared and was found on board one of the two little ships which stood in the harbor. Kendall had planned to sail back to England. A trial was held and he was hanged.

The houses were well started, but the food problem was growing worse each day. John Smith gathered everything he could find which could be used for trading goods and loaded it into a boat.

"Some of you get the fishnets into the water," he ordered. "There are plenty of oysters now, too, so we won't starve if you'll do a little work to get food. I am going up the river to an Indian village to trade for some grain for our bread."

No man questioned Smith's orders by now. When Ratcliffe gave him power to take over, John Smith made one rule. It was, "No work, no food." By now they knew that he meant it, and even Archer and the others who hated Smith followed his orders.

Smith chose a few men to go with him, and they rowed their boat up the river. The tribe in the village about twenty miles away had once been almost friendly. They had given the men plenty of beans, corn and berries for a little trading goods. But they had seen the white men lying about lazily. They had heard them fighting among themselves, and they knew that many had died at the time of the illness. They were no longer afraid of the white man's power.

When Smith's boat reached the riverbank near the village, the chief did not come down to meet the visitors. Only a few braves came down to see what Smith had in the boat. Then they went back to their storehouse and brought one small basket of grain.

John Smith looked down at it. "Is this all you can spare?" he asked.

The Indians looked him in the eye and laughed. "Our storehouse is full. But it is all the white man shall have for what he has brought."

In the boat were beads, copper, and hatchets, worth far more than the one small basket of corn. As the Indians watched, Smith seemed to grow to twice his size. He shoved away the little basket of corn so that it spilled on the riverbank.

"Get!" he cried in a voice that brought the Indians in the village out of their lodges. The Indians ran in terror, and John Smith fired his rifle over their heads. "Get, and don't come back until you have a boat-load of food to trade. And bring it down here to my boat!"

To make sure that his orders were followed, Smith marched up to the village. Indians scattered from his path. The other white men may have been like women, but this one was a man to fear!

Right to the chief's lodge marched Smith. He stooped to get inside the low door and then stood tall again to give his order to the chief. "You send six men, each carrying all the grain he can. And see that they are not wearing knives!"

The chief sent six men to the storehouse. Smith

followed them to the river and saw that his boat was loaded. Then he signalled the men with him to turn over the trading goods. There was a look of respect in the Indians' eyes as they watched John Smith push off for the trip back to James Fort.

The time of danger was over. With the work they had done and the food they had gathered, the men could live until Newport's ship returned. Life in America, thanks to John Smith, looked better.

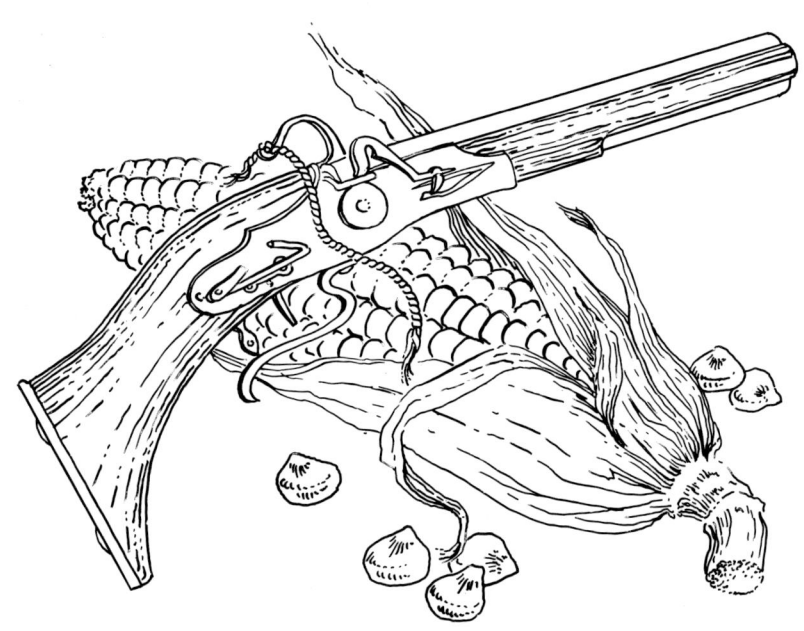

# CAPTURE OF JOHN SMITH

December came, and Captain Newport had not returned to James Fort. But all was going well. Most of the men even seemed to enjoy the hard work they did. Many had learned to swing an ax well, as they worked to cut firewood and logs to make the fort strong. John Smith's booming voice and bright eyes seemed to keep the whole camp cheerful.

When the work was well in hand, John Smith said one day, "I am going up the Chickahominy River to learn where it comes from. Who wishes to join me?"

Soon ten men were ready to go. They took one large boat and a dugout canoe, with food and ammunition to last several days. At an Indian village, they picked up two guides.

When they had gone as far up the river as the larger boat could go, Smith wanted to go a little farther. He was making a map of Virginia, and wanted to learn all he could.

"Three of us and the guides will go farther up stream in the canoe," he told the men. "There are unfriendly tribes near here, and it will be best if the rest of you wait right here near the river."

It was late in the afternoon when the men in the canoe reached the place where the Chickahominy started. John marked his map. When he had finished, it was too late to start back down the river to meet the other men.

"We'll camp here. I'll go into the woods to get a turkey or some kind of game to eat while you make camp," he said.

He took one of the guides and started into the woods. When the two men were quite a way from the river, they saw a likely looking place where they could wait quietly until game came into sight. Side by side, they crouched behind a fallen tree. There was no sound but the wind rattling the dry leaves on the oak trees.

The Indian raised his bow and fitted an arrow into place. John Smith's ears were slower in picking up the sound he had heard. A deer must be coming through the woods. He, too, took aim and waited.

Suddenly there was a cry such as no deer could make. Instantly, an Indian burst through the woods. John's gun roared, and the Indian fell.

The guide had lowered his bow, and was about to spring away from Smith when Smith grabbed him.

"No, you don't! You are going to keep on helping me, my friend," he muttered. "You are my shield." John Smith pulled the garter from one of his legs and used it to hold the Indian's left arm to his own. He could hear the cries of other Indians as they ran towards the place from which the gunshot had come. Using his right hand, he reloaded his gun. He held the Indian close with his left arm.

Again the gun boomed, and an Indian fell. The rest stopped, their arrows ready. To hit the great John Smith, they must go through the Indian. He was not of their own tribe, but the prize they wanted was the great soldier, not an Indian.

As soon as the second Indian fell, John began to reload with his right hand. It was slow work, made slower by the fact that he was backing away towards the place where he had left his friends and the canoe, dragging the frightened Indian with him.

The arrows soon flew. Smith's live shield became a dead weight. Once again, he managed to get the gun loaded and a third Indian fell. He did not dare turn his head to see if he were backing in the right direction. He could only hope. Step by step, he backed, wondering why his enemies did not circle him.

He soon learned why. He felt the ground soften under his feet. A few steps more, and he was knee deep in water. He almost fell backward. A quick look about told him he had backed into a great swamp.

"I'll have to make the best of this," he thought. "If they want me, they'll have to come in and get me."

He dropped the dead Indian and, backing until the water was over his waist, went on firing, reloading his gun as fast as he could. He was out of reach of the arrows, but no longer could his bullets hit the Indians, either. He saw the Indians talking together. Then, with a few keeping watch on Smith, the Indians set to work to make a campfire. Darkness was settling onto the swamp.

Now, with a chance to think, Smith could feel the ache where an arrow had struck his thigh. But before long, even that ache was gone, lost in a terrible chill that went through his whole body. The swamp water in December was very, very cold. With night, the

air, too, became chill and damp. Smith looked with longing at the campfire, even though it was circled by men who were waiting for a chance to kill him.

John Smith wondered about the men who had come with him. He could not know that it was because one had disobeyed his orders that he had been hunted down. Some of the men at the larger boat had wandered into the woods. Indians captured one, and questioned him.

"Where is the great one, the one you call Captain Smith?" they asked. Hoping to save his own life the man told them that Smith had gone up the river. Quickly a band had set out to find him. They found the canoe and killed the two men camping near it. It had taken only a short while to find John Smith.

At last John could stand the cold no longer.

"I'll die either way," he thought. "I may as well die warm and dry." He walked toward the campfire.

A month later, John Smith wondered that he could still be alive. He had been held under guard at the campfire that night, allowed to dry his clothes and well fed. The Indians had decided their prize was too good to kill without taking him to their chief.

He thought each day would be his last. His round, ivory pocket compass had saved his life when he went before the chief the first time.

"Magic!" he had said as he held the compass in his hand. The chief saw the needle swing until it stopped and pointed to John Smith. The captain made sure that he stood to the needle's north whenever he showed it.

"I am a chosen one of the sun and the stars and the moon," he told the chief. "The heavens will be angry at one who hurts me." The chief believed him and did not order Smith's death.

When the Indians took their prisoner to a lodge and fed him well every few hours, day and night, Smith thought they were fattening him up, planning to eat him. But all that happened was that he was taken on a journey from village to village and shown off. Seeing the only white man of whom they were afraid held as a prisoner, the chiefs decided to attack Jamestown.

John Smith was called before the chief and told of the plans. He thought quickly of how he could save his people.

"You have not learned all of the white man's

magic," he said. "Terrible things will happen to you if you try to hurt the men in the fort. More great birds have skimmed over the sea from the land of the rising sun. The Great Sun Spirit loaded onto the ships more magic to keep his Indian children from harming his white children. Even now, the new magic, stronger than any you have yet seen, waits in a box, pushing to get loose."

The chief was not sure what to do when he heard this. John Smith, thinking of Newport's promise to return with the ships, hoped that what he said was at least partly true.

The medicine men were called. Their fire was built in one of the larger lodges. As John was brought in, he could not see clearly at first, for the air was heavy with smoke which slowly trailed out the hole in the roof. When his eyes could see in the dimness, he made out a strange creature, sitting beyond the fire.

It looked like a heap of animals and birds until it moved. Then Smith saw that it was the medicine man. Half his body was painted red and half was black. Two large circles of white framed his eyes. His head was covered by a strange headdress. It was made of snake skins stuffed with moss and the furs of weasels all tied together by their tails. Where the tails met at the top of the medicine man's head, there was a crown of bird feathers.

As soon as Smith was seated the medicine man began to shake a gourd rattle. As he shook it, he sang in a sad, wailing way. Smith shivered as he heard it. Three more medicine men came in, dressed in feathers and skins and painted as the head man was. They joined in the sad song as they took places around the fire. Then three more joined them.

The song ended. The head medicine man laid down five grains of corn, beginning a circle around the fire to which he added five more grains after each song. This went on, hour after hour, until there were three circles of grain around the fire.

John Smith felt that he could not sit still another minute, but guards behind him touched him warningly whenever he tried to move a little. He hoped it was all over as the third circle was closed, but the medicine men did a strange dance and then began the singing again.

This time, when the song ended, a stick was laid

between two grains of corn in the outside ring. The sad singing began again. A stick was laid down a certain number of grains of corn from the first. It went on and on—a song, a stick, until the outer circle was all divided.

"What next?" John wondered. He was sure it was night by that time. All day, the only break in the ceremony had been the bringing of more wood for the fire. But now at last, the medicine men arose as if to say it was ended. Into the lodge came more Indians carrying bowls of food. John was given plenty to eat and drink along with the medicine men. Then they all lay down to sleep.

This went on for three days, a whirling wail of sound and movement.

"I'll go mad if there is another day of it," he thought. But the next day, he was led from the smoky lodge. He learned, a little later, that the ceremony had a special meaning. The fire was the sun. The circles around the "sun" were the Indians' land, and were the whole world to them. Beyond their land was the sea, and the whole was like a flat plate. The sticks meant the white man's guns coming into their land. The ceremony would protect the

Indian against the guns, they believed.

John was given something to do. They brought him a bag of gunpowder taken from a white captive. He was supposed to plant it in the ground, as the Indian planted corn, to make more gunpowder grow.

Smith shook his head. "I can plant it," he said, "but it will not grow unless the sun spirit smiles upon his Indian children as he does upon his white ones."

He made a show of planting the powder. Then there was more feasting, and at last came the day when he was taken to the village of the "king" of all the near-by tribes, the great chief Powhatan.

At Powhatan's village, John Smith was again treated well. While he waited to be called before the chief, he talked with the children who came to see him. He showed them strange things such as the buttons on his clothes and the way they fitted into the buttonholes. One who came often to watch was Powhatan's younger daughter, thirteen-year-old Pocahontas.

After several days, guards came for John Smith and led him to the large lodge of the great chief Powhatan.

The Indian leader was seated on a skin-covered platform at one end of the lodge. Powhatan wore a great robe of raccoon skins with a fringe of the striped tails. Pocahontas was seated on one side of him and her older sister on the other side. The Indian braves sat in two long rows on either side of the lodge, with the women behind them. All the braves wore special headdresses made of white bird's down, in honor of the day the fate of John Smith would be settled.

John knew his day had come. All through the ceremonies and the feasting, he felt eyes upon him. The eyes were mostly unfriendly, especially during the "pow-wow" before the throne after the bowls of food had been taken away.

When the braves went back to their places and several Indians carried in two large flat stones, John knew his fate. His life would end there on those rocks. He was led to the stones and ordered to put his head on one of them.

Pocahontas was talking with her father. She seemed to be begging for something, but he brushed her to one side. Powhatan stood ready to give a command. The braves picked up clubs which they had

brought with them. They fingered them now, in readiness for the moment when Powhatan's signal would let them beat John Smith to death.

Powhatan raised his hand. The Indians rushed forward. John closed his eyes to shut out the sight of the clubs. Then, as the men moved forward, there was a sharp cry, and John knew that Pocahontas had run forward and had thrown her body over his.

The warriors stepped back, waiting for Powhatan to order the girl away. Silence hung for a moment. Then there was one short sentence from Powhatan. The girl arose. John waited for the blows to fall. They never came.

# FOOTHOLD IN VIRGINIA

Powhatan did not change his mind again. John Smith was brought before him once more, but this time it was to order the white man to make chunks of copper, glass beads and good hatchets for the Indians. Because the Indians made everything they had from the materials around them, he thought that any white man could do the same.

"Good chief Powhatan, I would be most happy to make things for you," Smith said. "But I would have to go back to the fort to get the things. I will send them back to you if you will let me go back to my people."

Powhatan sent Smith back to his lodge without an answer. But two days later, Smith was taken to a place in the woods. Powhatan himself, dressed as fearfully as Indian art could make him, came to him there. There was another ceremony. At the end, Powhatan said, "Go to your people. Send us the things we want, and there shall be peace."

He wanted, besides the usual things, a pair of

grindstones and two guns. Smith said he should have them. He was to go home the next day, January 8, 1608, a month from the day he had left to go up the Chickahominy River.

During the night, a freezing rain came. The sun shone the next day on a woods bright with ice-coated branches, and ice crackling underfoot. Twelve guards went with Smith to James Fort.

The Indians waited outside the gate as surprised guards let John into the fort.

Mr. Hunt, the minister, came hurrying forward. "Smith! We gave you up for dead!" he cried. He and several others seemed truly glad to see John, but many others looked at John with hate in their eyes. Martin, his old enemy, had used every chance to plant the seeds of that hatred. Even Ratcliffe, who had looked to John Smith for help in leading the colony, was now cold toward him.

Before John could find out what had turned so many against him, he had to keep his promise to Powhatan. He pushed aside all who would stop him and took the two guns and had some of his friends help move the grindstones outside the gate. He filled an Indian basket with other trading goods.

Four of the braves were ready to carry away the grindstones. Two more reached for the guns, but John decided it would be best to see that they were empty before handing them over. He fired one at an icicle hung tree. The bits of ice rained to earth, tinkling like glass. He fired the other gun and then turned back to the Indians.

The grindstones were on the ground. The last of twelve Indians was disappearing behind a tree.

Smith waved his arms and yelled, "Come back! Powhatan will not let you come into your village without these!" The Indians must have had the same thought, for they turned when all was quiet and came back. Smith watched them go, carrying the gifts this time. Then he turned toward the fort, a free man at last.

But his freedom lasted only a few minutes. Archer, who had been a lawyer in England, walked towards him holding a paper. Ratcliffe held one of Smith's arms and Martin the other as other men put irons and chains onto Smith's ankles.

Archer put the paper into his hand. "What's this?" cried Smith. He saw that many men had signed the paper.

"For the death of the two men you left in the canoe on Chickahominy River. They lost their lives acting under your orders, and you did nothing to defend them. The law clearly states that you should pay for their lives."

The few men who were still John's friends cried out against the actions of the others. Ratcliffe and Martin were the only two councilmen other than Smith himself. They called a meeting, held a quick trial, and voted John Smith guilty. He was to be put to death.

There was to be no time of waiting, for Ratcliffe knew that John Smith was the strongest, smartest man among them. He would draw more and more men back to his side if he were given time.

"As the sun goes down tonight, he shall hang," Ratcliffe ordered. He put men to work at building a frame where the hanging could take place.

John Smith watched the sun drop lower and lower in the sky. He had been set free by the Indians, only to walk into a noose. His own people! And it was plain to see that little work had been done in this fort since the day he had left it! Had these men no sense? Too bad Captain Newport had not returned.

It was only an hour until sunset when a cry came from the watch at the corner of the fort.

"Sails ho!"

John Smith, in chains, was forgotten as the thirty-seven other men of the fort rushed to the watch towers to see the ships coming up the James River. The flag of England flew on the deck.

There was no hanging that night, or any other. Newport had had the chains taken from John Smith once before. Now, knowing that this was the man who had kept Jamestown alive, he took them off again with his own hands.

Captain Newport had brought one hundred twenty new settlers to live in Virginia. By April, when he sailed away again, James Fort was well on the way to becoming Jamestown, for new houses were soon being built outside the walls of the fort. John Smith was on hand to help with the chopping of trees and the cutting of boards.

The newcomers saw that in Smith they had their best leader, and elected him president in September.

A year later, there were women and children in Jamestown as well as men. Under Smith's leadership, and with the help of two more shiploads of people and goods brought by Newport, the colony had done well. There were almost five hundred people in Jamestown by September of 1609.

The Indian girl, Pocahontas, had come often to the colony in that year. She brought gifts of food whenever she came, and seemed to want to know the English people better. John Smith knew that without her friendship, Jamestown probably would have been wiped out by Powhatan.

All might have gone well from then on had not John Smith had to return to England. Coming down the James River one day that September, he was badly hurt when a keg of gunpowder exploded in the boat. Newport took him back to England where doctors could make him well again.

Without Smith to guide the trading with the Indians, the people of Jamestown had a bad winter. It was later called the "Starvation Time." They were not yet raising enough food for themselves, and Powhatan's friendship had weakened. Pocahontas tried harder than ever to get food to her new friends, and the colony managed to get through the winter.

A few years later, one of the colonists named John Rolfe married Pocahontas. It was John Rolfe who began to grow the Indian crop of tobacco to send back to England in trade for things the people of Virginia needed.

Others soon were doing the same, and Virginia became able to pay her own way. In a few years, the settlers rebuilt Jamestown on higher land away from the marshes which seemed to bring sickness to so many people. By then, the English people had a firm foothold in the New World.

Jamestown 1622

# MAYFLOWER DRIVEN TO NEW ENGLAND

It was five years before John Smith could go back to America. This time he did not go to Virginia, but to the land north of it which was called New England and belonged to a different trading company. He went partly to bring back a shipload of goods for that company and partly because he was a man who had to have adventures in his life.

Fishing was fine off the coast of New England. While the crew filled the ship's hold with fish, John Smith followed the shoreline. He marked the shape of the land on a map, and the places where there were Indian villages near the shore. He learned what he could of rivers whose mouths he saw. When he sailed back to England, he had made a fine map for the people who would come later.

John showed his map to King James. The king's son, fifteen-year-old Prince Charles, was very much interested in it.

"We shall name the places in New England after places here in old England," he decided. He wrote names onto the map, *Plymouth, London, Oxford* and *Dartmouth* where there were Indian villages. He named the big, hook-like arm of land which reached out into the sea *Cape James,* for his father, and some islands for Captain Smith. He named a river *Charles River,* after himself. Most of the names were changed later, but *Charles River* is on the map today. *Cape James* soon became *Cape Cod,* the fisherman's name for it.

On a November day in 1620, a wooden ship moved steadily toward Cape Cod. On board were ninety-eight men, women and children, besides the sailors, and every one of them worn and tired from a journey which had been too long in getting underway. When they had finally got away from the English port of Plymouth, the season of fall storms was close.

There had been a bad one in mid-ocean. As the ship was thrown against the waves, a terrible sound made each one sure that the ship was splitting apart. It almost did, for a great crack appeared in the center beam, and it had taken all the men's strength and the jack screw out of a printing press to patch it.

Land was a welcome sight to Captain Jones. He

would make no money on this trip. He would be lucky to get his ship and his sailors back to England without all of them starving to death or dying of the scurvy.

His passengers called themselves Pilgrims—people traveling because of religion. They had tried to separate from the Church of England, and to do that was against the law in those days. In northern Virginia, where they were heading with a land grant from the London Company, they hoped to live apart from the Jamestown settlers and be able to have a church of their own.

Captain Jones checked his maps, including the new one drawn by John Smith. They were too far north! He would have to follow that dimly seen shoreline southward, for it appeared to be Cape James or Cape Cod, as the seamen called it. The London Company land began just south of the Hudson River.

While the Pilgrims looked longingly at the dark shoreline to the west, sailors scurried up the rope ladders and pulled at the ropes that moved the sails. The ship swung southward.

As the setting sun changed the color of the waves

so that a man's eyes could not tell water from rock, the Pilgrims kneeled on the deck for evening prayers. But their prayers were suddenly ended as they heard a horrible scraping sound. The *Mayflower* stopped, and listed horribly to one side. The ship's mate called out orders and the sailors scurried to the rigging again, furling this sail, turning that one. The ship must back off the rocks and sand on which it hung, and quickly, or it would be wrecked.

The prayers began again as the ship hung there. As if in answer, a breeze swung up from the southwest. With a great shudder, the *Mayflower* pulled free and headed to the north and the east, well out into deep water.

"We'll not make it south to Virginia," Captain Jones said. "We shall head for a safe harbor, and the nearer the better."

Nothing William Bradford, one of the stronger young men among the Pilgrims, could say would change Captain Jones' mind. They dared not say so, but most of the Pilgrims felt the Captain was right. The sooner they could anchor the ship, the better, no matter what land they were near.

"Where the Lord sends this ship is where we

should go," said Mr. Carver, a leader among the Pilgrims.

"Amen," said some of the others.

The *Mayflower* swung south around the hook of Cape Cod until she was safely inside a curving arm of land.

"Find the place where you will build your houses," said Captain Jones. "The *Mayflower* can't make it back to England now, so find a place where there is a good harbor, too."

Land, whether in Virginia or not, felt good under the feet that had walked the ship's boards so many weeks. The women could hardly wait to get to a pond of fresh water where they could wash their families' clothes. The men, led by the soldier who had come with them, Miles Standish, set off on foot to explore the hills of Cape Cod.

The ship's carpenter went to work putting the shallop into good condition. The shallop was a sailboat big enough to carry twenty men. The Pilgrims had brought it with them in the hold of the Mayflower. When it was ready, the men set out on a longer exploring trip.

On their first trip out, the men had seen a few

Indians. Miles Standish wanted to trade with them for some of their corn, but they ran at the sight of the white men. When they found a mound with corn buried in it, the Pilgrim men took several of the Indians' baskets full of the yellow, red and blue kernels.

"We shall pay them for it when we can," they said.

They saw the Indians on their next trips away from the *Mayflower,* but there was no chance to pay for the corn. The Indians' arrows were their greeting, and the Pilgrims' guns answered back.

Through freezing rain they moved on in their boat in search of a place away from such unfriendly neighbors. They followed the curve of Cape Cod and headed northward. There they found the place that seemed right to them. The water was deep enough to anchor the *Mayflower* in the harbor. There was a small river which they named Jones River after their ship's captain, and there was a patch of ground where the stubble of old corn still stood.

"Indians lived here at one time, but there is no sign of them now," Miles Standish said. "I am in favor of this as our building place."

"Aye," said the others, and they carried the good

news back to the *Mayflower.* The ship moved across the bay and around an arm of land into the harbor the men had found. December 24, 1620, she lay at anchor there and, on Christmas Day, the Pilgrims went ashore in the ship's small boat.

Captain Jones looked at his copy of John Smith's map.

"Prince Charles named this place Plymouth," he told the people.

"Plymouth it shall stay," said Mr. Carver, who had been elected governor of the colony. "Plymouth is a good English name."

It seemed right that the journey which had begun at Plymouth in old England should end at Plymouth in New England.

They began the work of building houses along the street they laid out on a rise of land above the beach. And they wondered about the Indian village which had once been on that spot. They did not know that Captain Smith had found the village in his explorations, and had made friends with the tribe that lived there. But after he left, the captain of another ship which had come with Smith's ship went on shore there. He invited Indians to come on board his ship to trade and then sailed away with them.

He took his Indian captives to Spain, where he sold them as slaves. But one of them, whose name was Tisquantum or Squanto, as he is usually called, was taken to England. There a man who was about to explore the New England coast found him. The man was Captain Dermer, who took Squanto with him to be his guide.

The Pilgrims, as they chose their land, did not know that Captain Dermer had been there earlier that same year, and that he had reported Plymouth as a fine place for a settlement. But Squanto, back at his old home, had found none of his tribe there. He learned that soon after he and the other Indians had been taken captive, a sickness had come to the tribe and killed almost everyone. Captain Dermer, seeing how the near-by tribes hated the Englishmen because of the kidnapping, had done all he could to try to make friends. He had given Squanto his freedom before he headed south to Virginia.

Governor Carver decided that the first building should be a storehouse and meeting room to be used by all the people. It was to be about twenty feet square. Men who had never before swung an ax worked until muscles ached and hands were blistered. But with everyone working together, the storehouse was finished. The sailors began to bring the Pilgrims' goods ashore.

"Indians!" the cry went up one day. The men dropped their axes and picked up their guns. But the Indians ran away as soon as they knew they had been seen.

One day, some tools were left where the men had been cutting trees. They were gone the next day when someone went after them. The Pilgrims had an uneasy feeling that they were being watched.

The houses had just been begun when work had to stop. During January and February a sickness, which had begun even before they reached Plymouth, brought death to one Pilgrim family after another. William Mullins' whole family except his daughter, Priscilla, died. Miles Standish lost his wife, as did several other men. By March, about half the Pilgrims and half the sailors were dead. The Pilgrims who were left hid the graves by planting a field above them to hide from the Indians how many had died.

One day in March, when the Pilgrims were back

at work on their houses, they saw an Indian coming toward their village. He did not stop on a near-by hillside to stare, but marched right down into town.

"Welcome, Englishmen!" he said, in quite clear English.

The Pilgrims, when they got over their surprise, learned that Captain Dermer had taught this man his English. The captain had brought him from Maine to Cape Cod.

"Me Samoset," he told the Pilgrims. "Me friend to Englishmen."

Samoset's coming was the turning point for the Pilgrims. It was he who brought Squanto to them a few days later. Squanto brought the chief, Massasoit, to talk with the Pilgrims, and not to fight. Then, when a peace treaty had been signed, Squanto decided to stay with the Pilgrims to teach them how to live in the wilderness.

"We should be planting our seeds," said those who had farmed in England.

"Soon, perhaps," said Squanto. "Plant the seeds which can live through freezing cold which still may come. But the corn must not be planted until the leaves of the white oak are as large as a mouse's ear."

When that day came, Squanto showed the Pilgrims how his people had grown corn in those same fields. He picked up dead fish washed from the sea and placed a fish in each of the holes he dug. The rotting fish helped feed the soil.

Captain Jones had set sail for England with what was left of the *Mayflower* crew in April. As the Pilgrims watched the sails disappear, they felt very much alone. There were fishing boats of both English and French people farther to the north, and there was a French settlement far away at Quebec. Many miles to the south was Jamestown. But the only real neighbors the Pilgrims had were the Indians. It was well that they had Squanto to help them keep peace with the red men and to teach them how to find food.

In the early summer, Governor Carver died, and William Bradford was chosen governor in his place.

"The new governor should send his good wishes to Chief Massasoit," Squanto told the Pilgrims. "There are tribes who go to Massasoit with words of hate for the Englishmen. They tell him the Englishmen stole the corn of the red man as soon as they came from over the sea."

Governor Bradford said, "I will send gifts to Massasoit. And we must let him know that we wanted to buy that corn and we will pay for it."

He sent Stephen Hopkins and Edward Winslow, with Squanto as a guide. They took beads, some chain, and a very special red coat as gifts. They found the chief. He put on the coat and hung the chain around his neck. He seemed very proud. He offered the visitors tobacco, but he had no food.

He told Squanto to tell the white men they could sleep on the chief's bed.

"Thank him for us, Squanto," said Winslow. But he and Hopkins got little sleep that night, for they had to share the bed with Massasoit, his wife, and two other Indian men.

The next day, the chiefs under Massasoit came to meet the Englishmen. Fishermen brought in two large fish about noon, but there were forty people to feed, so the Pilgrims were very hungry when they left the village. They returned to Plymouth, more thankful than ever for what they had there.

Massasoit called for the Englishmen's help a few weeks later. Miles Standish quickly went to the village where Corbitant, Massasoit's enemy, lived. With his big gun, he frightened Corbitant's men into calling off their attack.

In the fall, when the crops were gathered and the hunting was good, the Pilgrims invited Massasoit and ninety of his men to feast with them. They had much to be thankful for, and made it a feast of Thanksgiving.

Among their blessings, they counted the friendship of Squanto and the goodness of Captain Dermer, who had taught the Indians that Englishmen could be their friends.

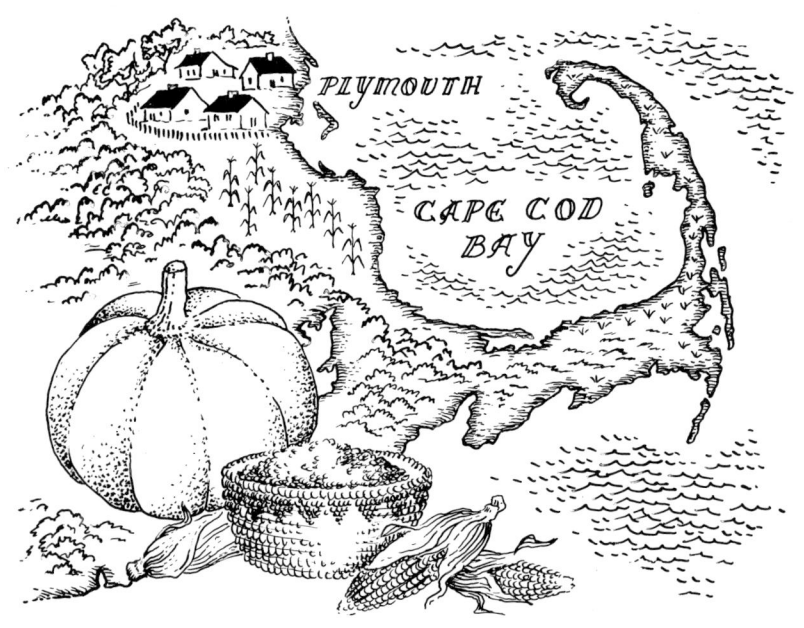

# PLYMOUTH STANDS FIRM

Had the Pilgrims known what was to come, they would have laid in even larger stores of food. Soon after the Thanksgiving Feast, the Pilgrims were surprised to see a ship coming into the bay. It was the *Fortune*. On board were thirty-five people who had come to join the Pilgrims at Plymouth.

"We will help you bring your supplies from the ship," said Miles Standish.

One of the newcomers laughed and said, "We have little more than the poor clothing on our backs."

"Surely you brought supplies to last the winter!" said Governor Bradford.

The people shook their heads. "No. We thought that in this land of plenty we could find enough to carry us over until we plant our fields in the spring."

The *Fortune* sailed away two weeks later. The food which had seemed plenty now had to feed twice as many people. Game was not easy to get in the winter months, and again the Pilgrims knew a time of hunger.

One day, an Indian runner came into the village. He was not of Massasoit's people, but was from the other side of the bay. He came to Governor Bradford and handed him a snakeskin filled with arrows. Then he turned and left the village.

"Squanto, what does this mean?" asked Governor Bradford.

Squanto looked at the evil-looking bundle. "It is a warning," he said. "It means the tribes will attack."

The Pilgrim leaders saw fear on each other's faces. Miles Standish saw it as he came into the room.

"Don't let the Indians think we are afraid," he said. "Here's their answer." He tossed the arrows to one side and stuffed the snakeskin with bullets.

A messenger was sent to deliver it, but he was soon back still carrying it. The Indians had refused to touch it.

Miles Standish lost no time in getting all the men to work cutting logs to build a palisade around the Plymouth houses. Then they built a strong, square building up on Murdock's Hill just above the village. They put their cannons on the roof and built up protecting walls. The lower story, they thought, could be a church when it was not needed as a place of safety.

Summer came, and as yet there had been no attack. "We called their bluff," Miles Standish said. But trouble of another kind came. A ship arrived, again with a load of people and no supplies for them. But these were not more Pilgrims who had come to join their friends at Plymouth. The sixty men who came this time were rough adventurers.

They laughed when the pilgrims said they had little food to spare. They went into the cornfields where the ears were still green. They pulled the ears from the stalks and helped themselves to everything they wanted. Miles Standish and some of the other men finally drove them out of Plymouth. They headed northward, supposedly to start a trading town.

"Another hungry winter is ahead for us," said Governor Bradford. "It is far too late to plant another corn crop."

"I'll go to the Indian villages and try to trade for some of theirs," Miles Standish said.

As he made his trips to visit the tribes a little later, when the corn crop had ripened, Captain Standish heard stories of the newcomers.

"These Englishmen rob us in the night!" the Indians told him. "They do not build houses, Captain Standish. They sleep in tents, and lie about all day, waiting for the night when they can steal more."

Standish learned that the men did some hunting and fishing, but they were not clearing fields to plant corn in the spring. Soon there began to be a different feeling when Standish went into the Indian villages. Even Massasoit seemed less friendly.

That fall, the Pilgrims lost their good friend Squanto, who died. Another Indian, named Hobamok, had come to live with them, but they missed their old friend.

By March, the bad feelings toward the newcomers had spread to all white men. Miles Standish went to a village farther south along the bay to trade for corn. He took the shallop to the shore near the village and went up to the chief's house. Two Indians from another tribe were there, talking with the chief. Standish could not understand what they were saying, but he knew they were talking about him.

Soon they called in a fourth Indian and talked

with him. This man turned to Captain Standish, and began to act very friendly.

"I shall help carry your corn," he said, and did so. Then he said, "Oh, honored Englishman, bravest of soldiers, that is not enough corn for one so fine as you. I shall give you more from my own fields."

He brought down a large kettle of corn and put it into the shallop. By that time, darkness was near.

"Come to my lodge to sleep, Captain," he said. "I shall not rest well unless you do."

"No, thank you," said Standish. "I shall stay by my boat."

"Then I, too, shall stay here to keep you company," said the Indian.

Standish built a fire. All night he lay near it, wide awake. The Indian waited and waited for the captain to sleep so that he could follow his orders to kill the man and bring back all the corn.

When Standish got into the shallop at dawn and headed back to Plymouth, the Indian followed on the shore. He was always near Plymouth in the next weeks, but Standish did not give him the chance he waited for.

Word came that Massasoit was dying. Knowing

that the Indians expected all their friends to visit at such a time, Governor Bradford sent Edward Winslow, with the Indian Hobamok and another Pilgrim to see the old chief. When they reached Massasoit's lodge, they found the medicine men there. All the people were gathered, singing a song of death.

When they had finished, someone told Massasoit his friend, Edward Winslow, had come. The sick man motioned for Winslow to come near.

Winslow stepped to the side of the couch. The old Indian reached out his hand and Winslow took it. The Pilgrim could hardly hear the old man when he spoke.

"Keen Winsnow?"

Winslow knew the Indians could not say his name correctly, and that the chief was asking, "Are you Winslow?"

He answered in the Indian word for yes, "Ahhe."

"Matta need woncanet namen, Winsnow," murmured the old chief. "I shall never see you again, Winslow." The sight seemed to have gone from his eyes.

Winslow called Hobamok and asked him to tell the chief that he brought things which he thought would help. The chief seemed pleased. He willingly sipped the fruit juices Winslow had brought, and asked for some of the English soup he had once tasted. Winslow cooked the best soup he could with what he could find to make it.

The Indians were pleased and surprised to see their dying chief grow stronger. Before Winslow left to go back to Plymouth, Massasoit called him to his side.

With Hobamok's help, the chief told Winslow that he had been asked to join other tribes in war against the English. He had believed the stories that the English had become his enemy, and was ready to send his men to war when he fell ill.

"Now I know you are my true friends," he said. "I tell you what you must do to save yourselves. Do not wait for attack. Go now to the village of the Massachusetts tribe and kill their chiefs."

Winslow and his two companions hurried back to Plymouth. They told the council of Massasoit's advice, and Miles Standish got ready to go to the villages to the north of Plymouth. He took eight men in the shallop and set out.

Massasoit had said that the Massachusetts tribes

planned to kill all that were left of the sixty traders first. Many had already been killed. Some had been taken as slaves to the Indians, for they would do anything to get food. Some had died of illness. Miles Standish and his men went ashore near their camp first of all. It was at the southern edge of what is now Boston Harbor.

"Go back to Plymouth," he told the weak handful of men who were there. "We shall give you seed corn to start again, and help you until it is grown."

An Indian scout from the Massachusetts villages saw Standish and his men. He hurried back to his chiefs to tell them that the soldier had an angry look in his eye. Four of the Massachusetts chiefs came down to the white men's camp, pretending to be on a trading trip for the furs they brought with them.

Pecksuot, the biggest of the chiefs, walked up to Miles Standish, who was strong but not very tall. Looking down at Standish, Pecksuot said, "You are a great captain, but you are a little man. I am not the greatest of chiefs, but I am a man of great strength and courage."

He spoke in his own tongue, and Hobamok repeated his meaning to Standish. Miles Standish said nothing, but he made his plans.

The next day, the four chiefs and Standish and four of his men were all inside a lodge. At a signal from Standish, one man leaped to guard the door while each of the others grabbed a chief. Standish jumped for Pecksuot.

Pecksuot's knife hung on a cord around his neck. It was pointed like a needle and both edges were ground thin. As Standish held his arms, the Indian did his best to get hold of the knife. The two strong men struggled, each trying his best to hold the other off and yet get the knife himself.

"Little man, am I?" grunted Standish. With a sudden, quick movement, he let go of the Indian's left arm and seized the knife before Pecksuot could get it. A moment later, the big Indian lay dead.

Each white man had been struggling in the same way, and each got his man down. Hobamok stood to one side, watching the terrible struggles. When only the Englishmen stood, he turned to Standish, respect in his eyes.

He said, "Yesterday Pecksuot bragged of what a big man he was. Today you have shown that you are big enough to lay him on the ground."

Before Standish and his men returned to Plymouth, there was one more short fight. This one, too, was settled without guns, and the Englishmen were the winners.

"If the white man can put down our chiefs without his gun, what can we do against him in war?" they thought. Instead of attacking Plymouth, they let the Pilgrims live peacefully.

There was no way for them to know it, but that spring of 1623 marked the end of the Pilgrims' great troubles. Their crops grew well. Ships came from England bringing more supplies and more good people.

Plymouth stood solid and firm, for the one thing they needed most they had with them all the time. That was courage.

New colonies in America came fast after 1623. The Dutch people had already begun sending fur traders up the river which Henry Hudson had found for them. A village was begun where Albany, New York, now stands. Before 1630, New York, the city which was to become the largest of American cities, had its start. The Dutch called it New Amsterdam.

But most of the colonies which grew along the

Atlantic coast between Florida and Maine were English colonies. In time, even New York was taken over by England. These were the people who were to be the builders of a new nation, the United States of America.

Without the courage of those who dared to settle on a strange shore, there would be no United States of America.